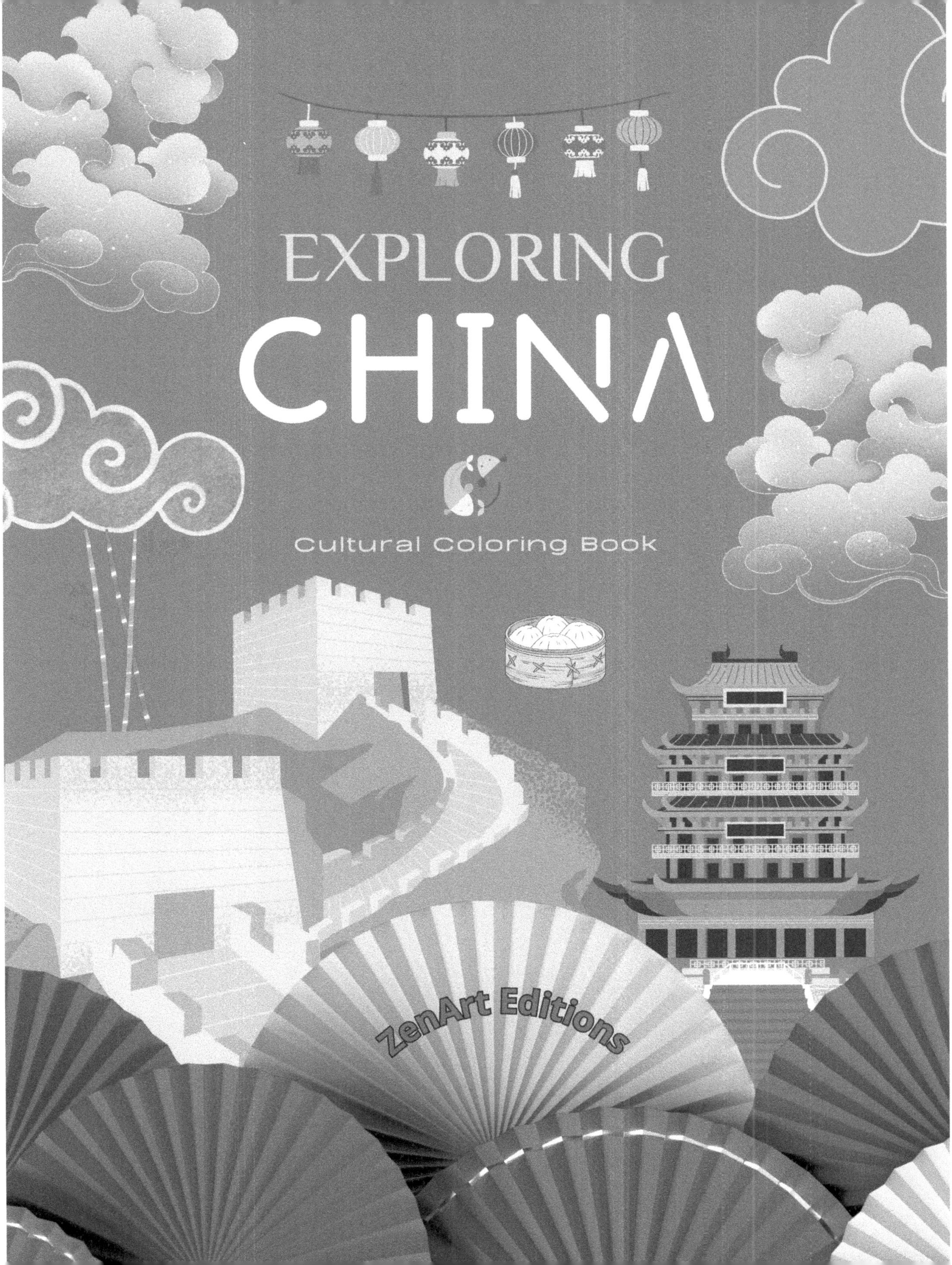
EXPLORING
CHINA
Cultural Coloring Book
ZenArt Editions

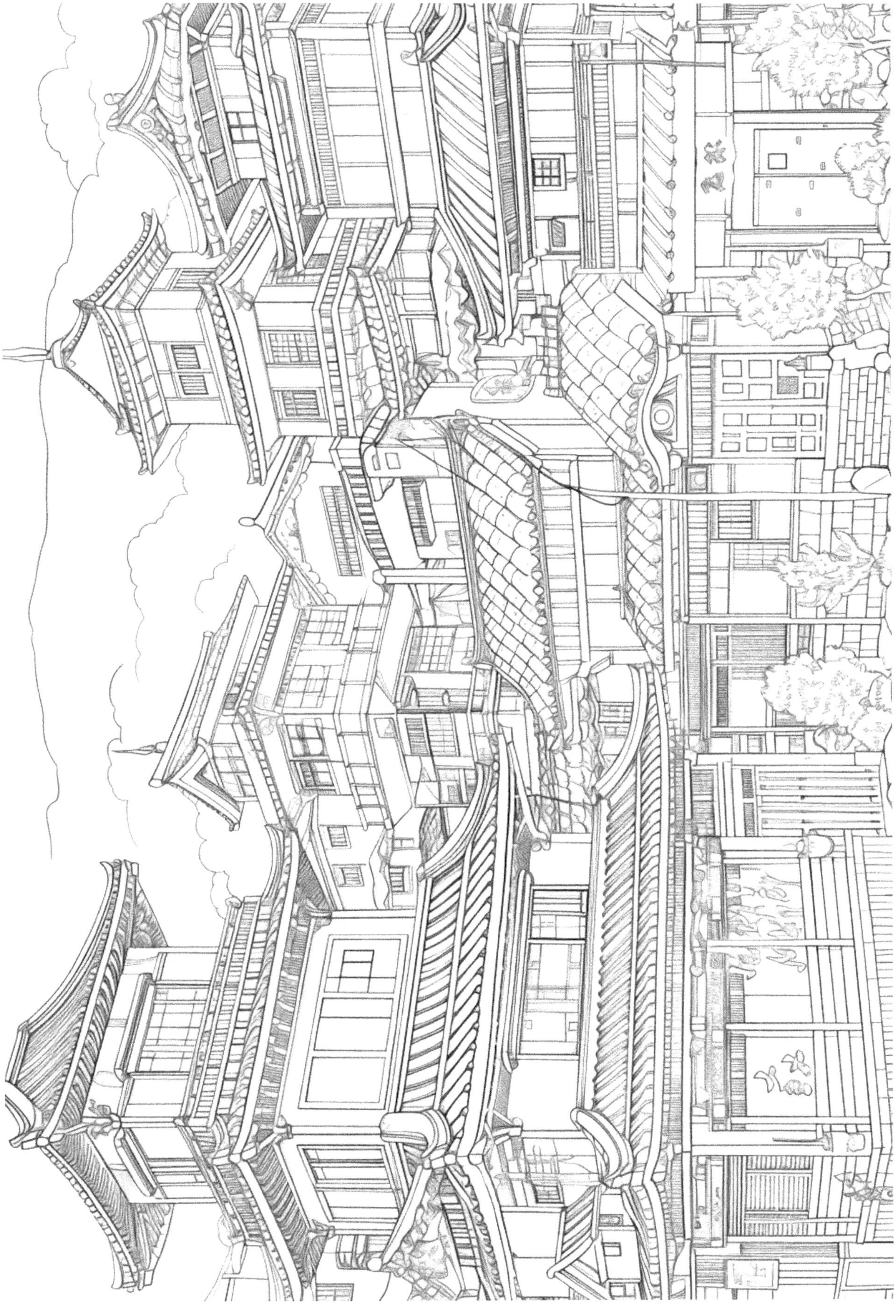

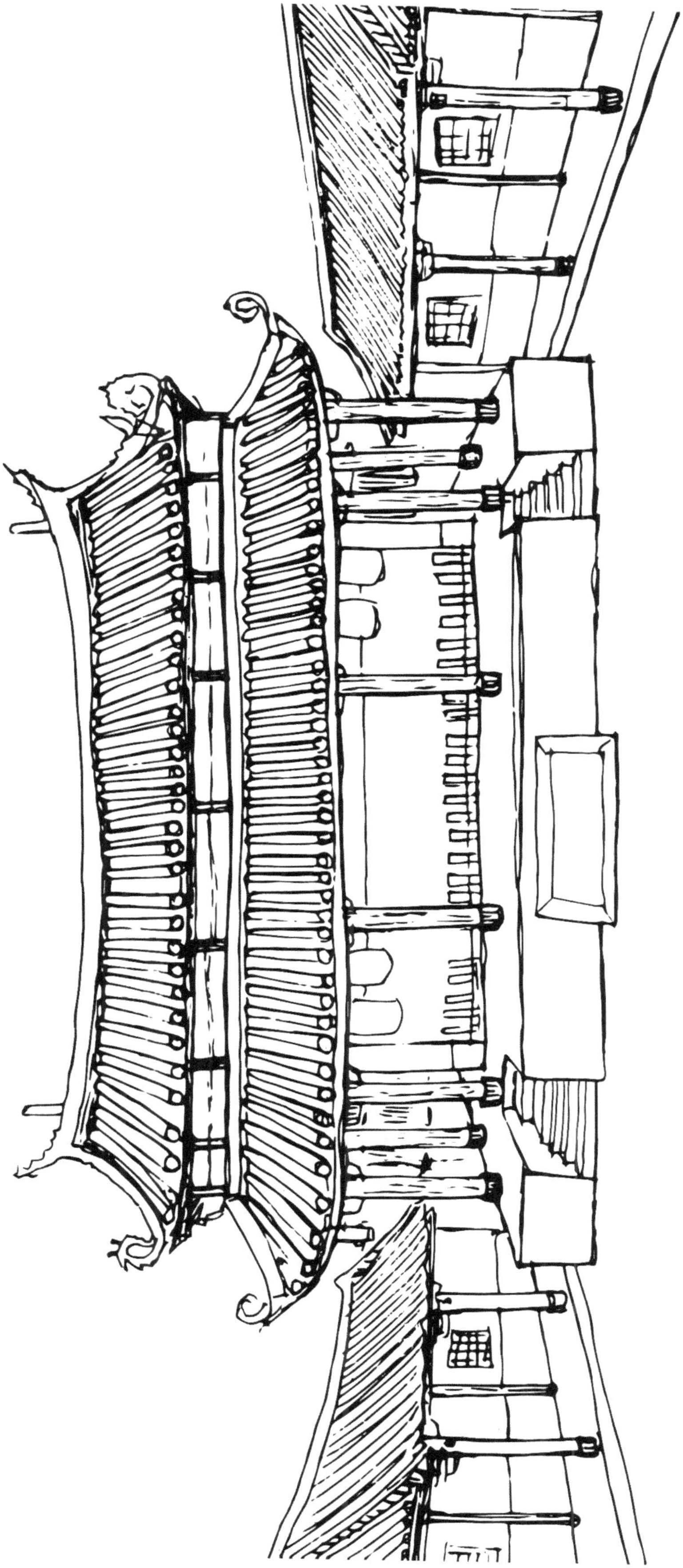

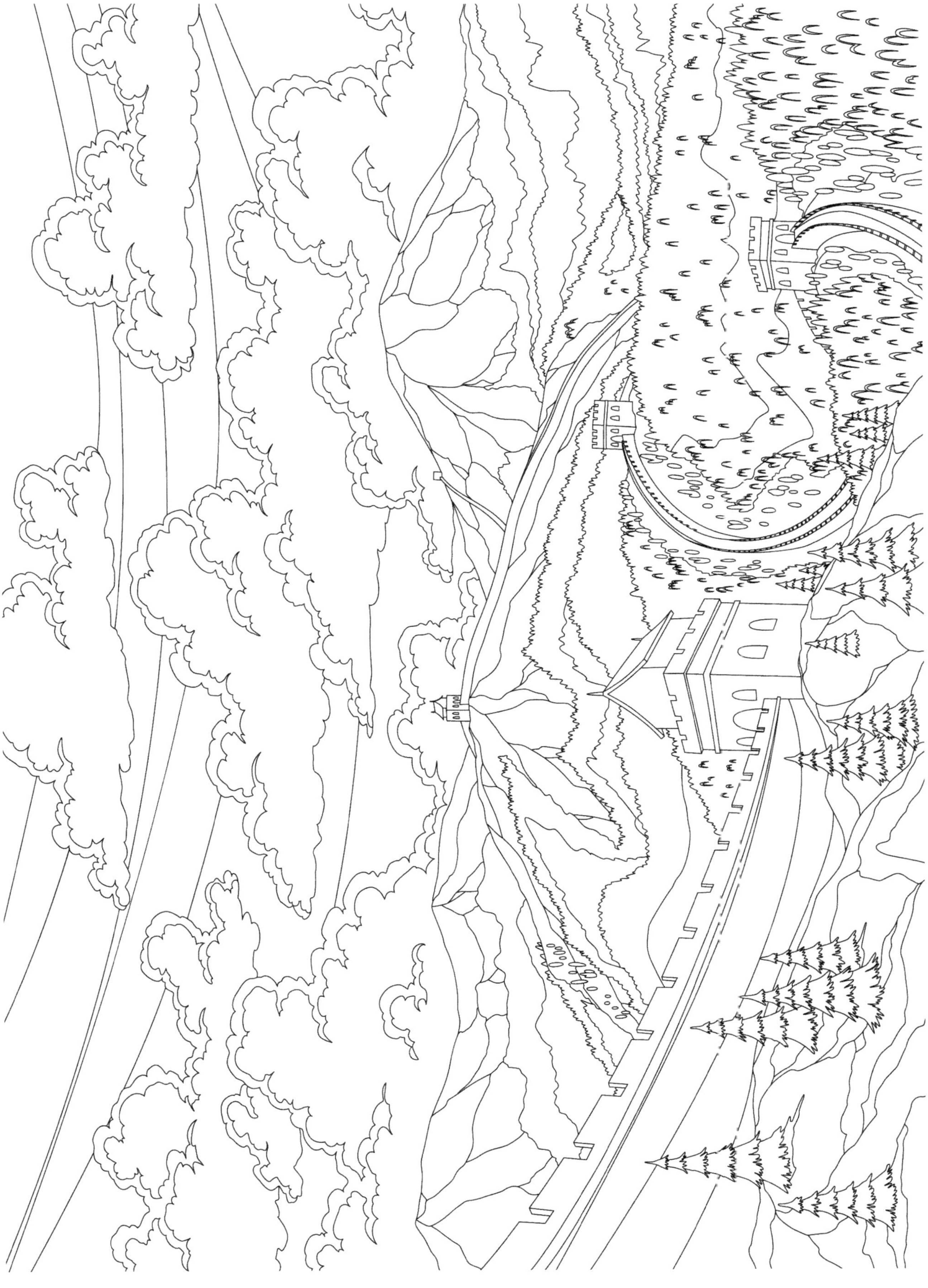

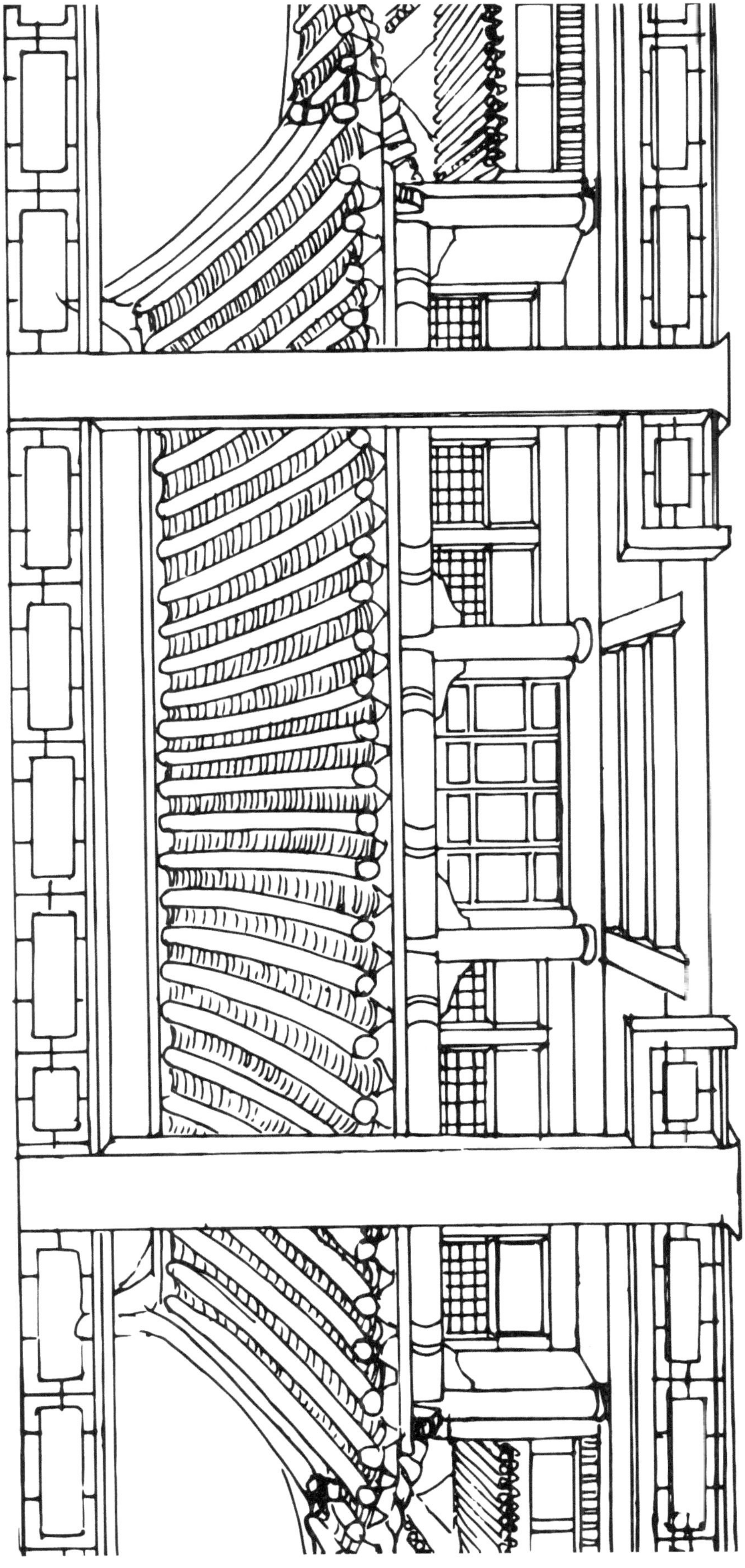

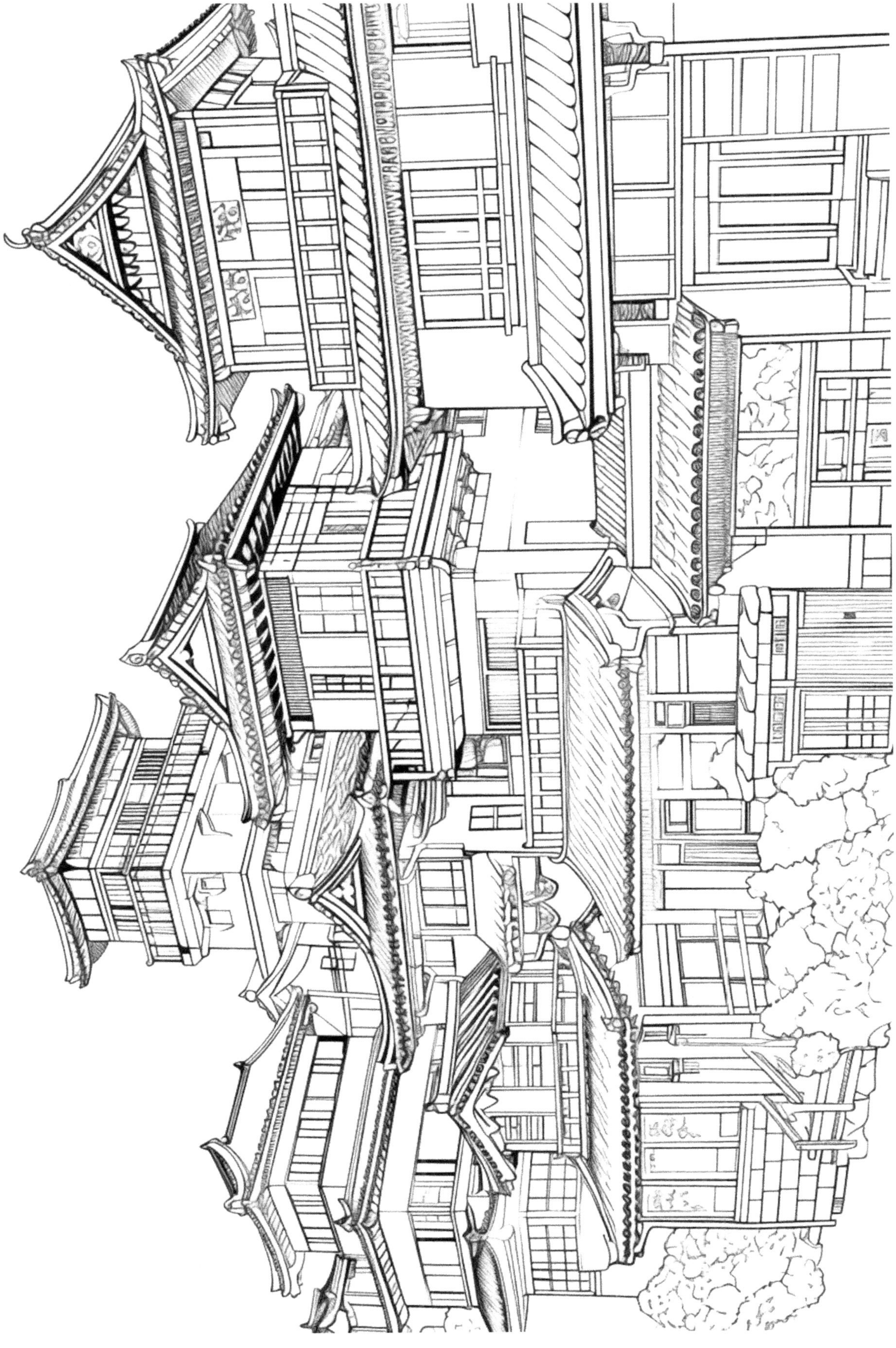

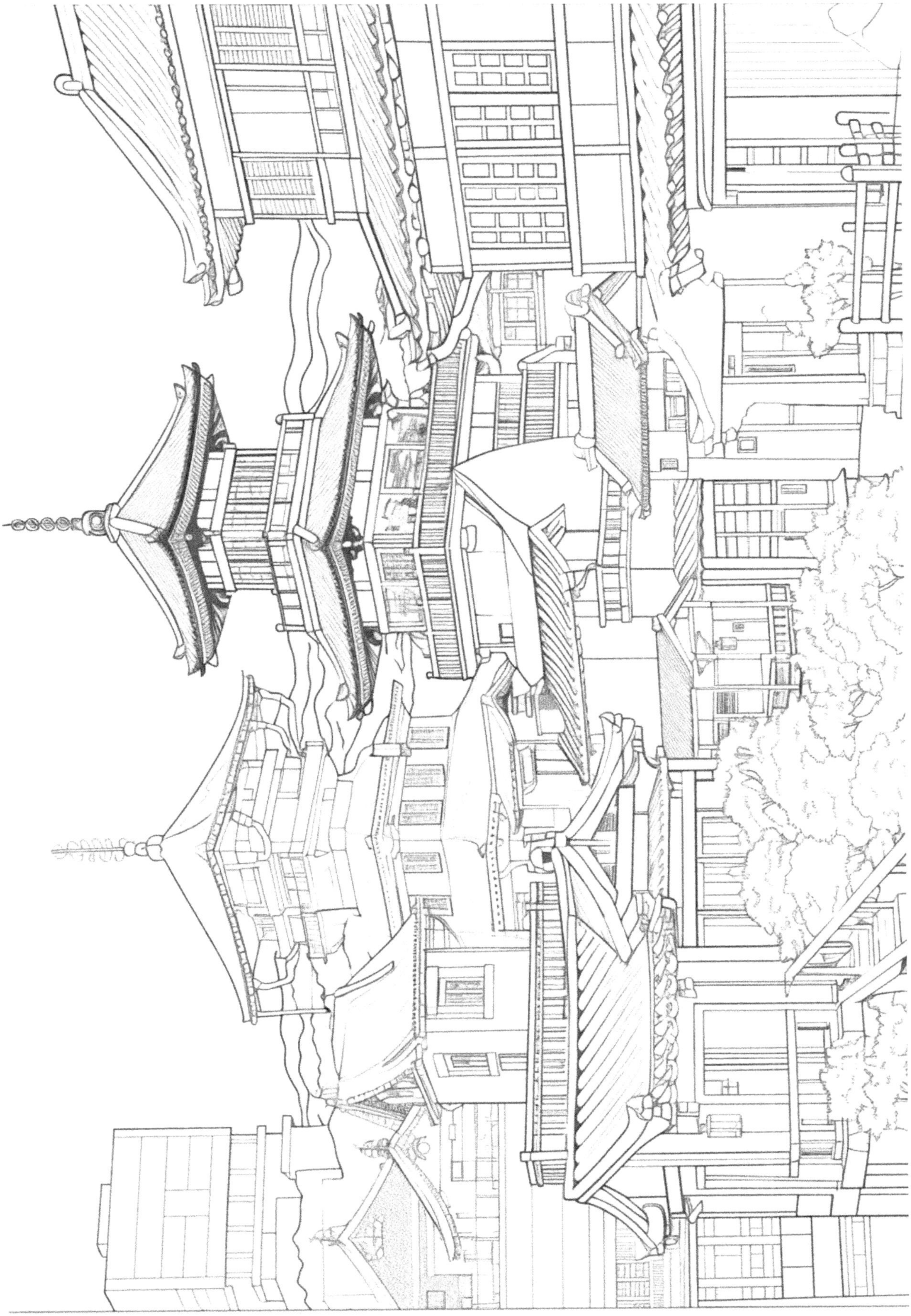

Milton Keynes UK
Ingram Content Group UK Ltd.
UKHW050353281123
433389UK00008B/364

9 798210 827814